WEATHER ALERT!

CONTENTS

T0362837

WEATHER ALERT!

Most communities have a meteorological service. Met services gather information about the weather and inform and alert people as to what may happen to the weather in the next few days.

Many people rely on the work of met services. Farmers rely on weather forecasts to know when to plant or harvest crops. Airlines, fisheries, tourism operators and builders also need to know what sort of weather to expect. People use weather forecasts to plan trips to the beach or the snow.

Weather forecasts also warn people about extreme weather events such as thunderstorms, cyclones and tornadoes. This is a very important function. Emergency services, such as ambulance services and bushfire brigades, can then prepare for trouble. With advanced warning, people can take precautions to save their property and even their lives.

MANY PEOPLE RELY ON THE WORK OF MET SERVICES.

TRACKING THE BIG ONES

PREDICT

What do you think this chapter will be about?

Meteorologists are able to predict and track thunderstorms, tornadoes and cyclones as they develop and move around the world. Satellites orbiting the Earth send pictures and radar images, which show the swirling, cloud patterns. Radar aboard ships and aeroplanes also give meteorologists valuable information about the formation and location of extreme weather events.

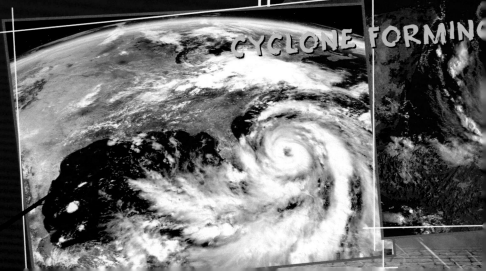

CYCLONE FORMING

INFORMATION

Tropical cyclones are the largest
of all windstorms, and have
different names in different parts
of the world. They are known as
hurricanes in the West Indies
and North America, as typhoons
in India, China and Japan, and
as cyclones in Australia and the
South Pacific.

WATCH THIS SPACE...

THUNDERSTORM!

Up to 50,000 thunderstorms occur in the world every day. Thunderstorms develop from tall, puffy clouds called cumulonimbus clouds. When a body of cold air (a cold front) flows over a body of warmer air (a warm front), the warm air flows upwards at great speed. The top of a thunderstorm cloud may soar more than ten kilometres into the air.

A thunderstorm is classified as 'severe' if it has one or both of the following features:

- hailstones more than two centimetres wide
- wind gusts of more than 90 kilometres per hour.

cumulonimbus

cold air

strong updraught

strong downdraught

warm air

heavy rain

strong updraught

FORMATION OF A THUNDERSTORM

CUMULONIMBUS CLOUDS

loud

cold front

strong
downdraught

strong gusts of wind

Synonym =
A word or phrase that
has the same meaning as
another word or phrase

severe

Which is the correct synonym?

A   dangerous

B   harsh

C   mild

A, B or C ?

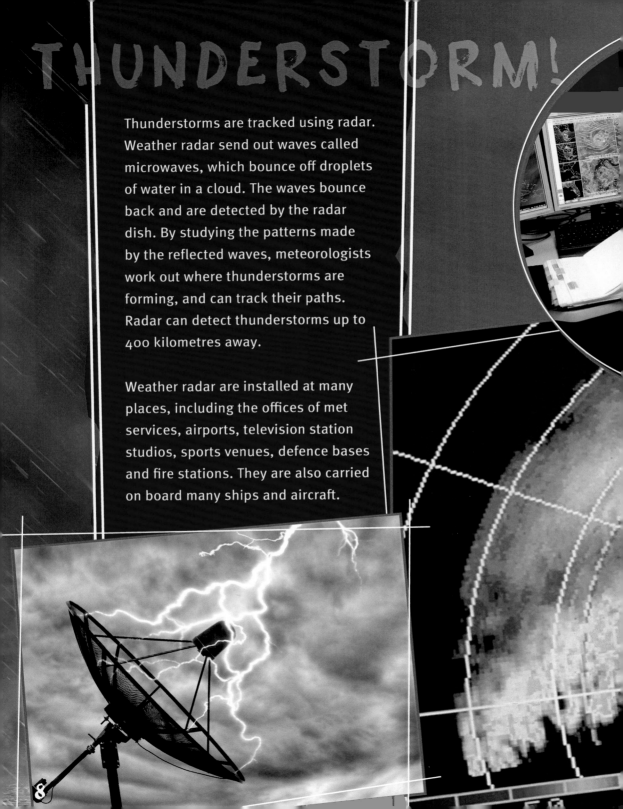

THUNDERSTORM!

Thunderstorms are tracked using radar. Weather radar send out waves called microwaves, which bounce off droplets of water in a cloud. The waves bounce back and are detected by the radar dish. By studying the patterns made by the reflected waves, meteorologists work out where thunderstorms are forming, and can track their paths. Radar can detect thunderstorms up to 400 kilometres away.

Weather radar are installed at many places, including the offices of met services, airports, television station studios, sports venues, defence bases and fire stations. They are also carried on board many ships and aircraft.

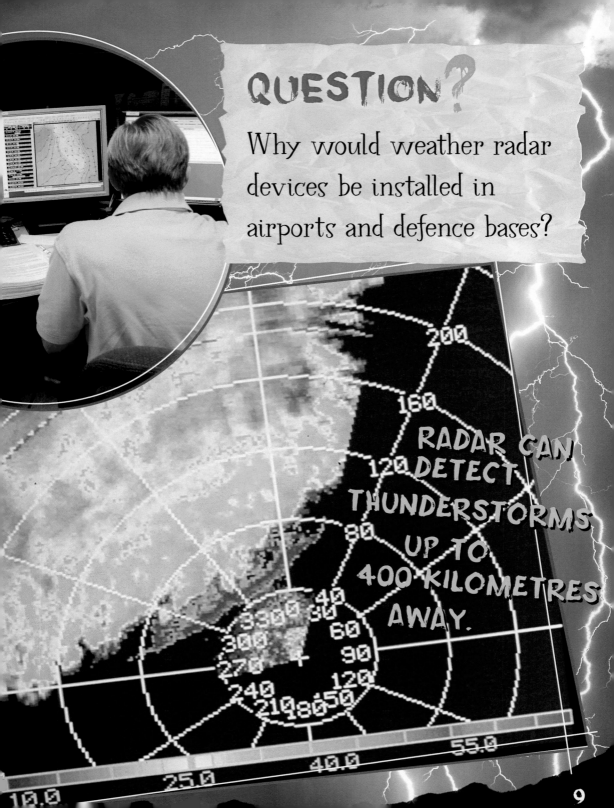

Why would weather radar devices be installed in airports and defence bases?

200

160

RADAR CAN
120 DETECT
THUNDERSTORMS
80 UP TO
400 KILOMETRES
AWAY.

40
330 30
300 60
270 90
240 120
210 180 150

10.0 25.0 40.0 55.0

THUNDERSTORM ALERT!

Once a thunderstorm has been detected, meteorologists track its progress on their radar screens. Other information comes from passing aircraft or ships, and from people close to the storm. If the storm is a severe one and likely to cause damage, a thunderstorm warning will be issued. Radio stations broadcast the warning to their listeners. If the storm is very severe, television stations will also broadcast a warning. Emergency services, such as ambulance, police and rescue workers, get ready to help out in case they are needed.

A thunderstorm warning may warn about the four main dangers associated with thunderstorms. Heavy rain may cause flash flooding. Hail may destroy crops, damage cars and buildings, and injure people. Lightning may injure or kill people. High winds may damage buildings or blow down trees.

TRACK

EVACUATE

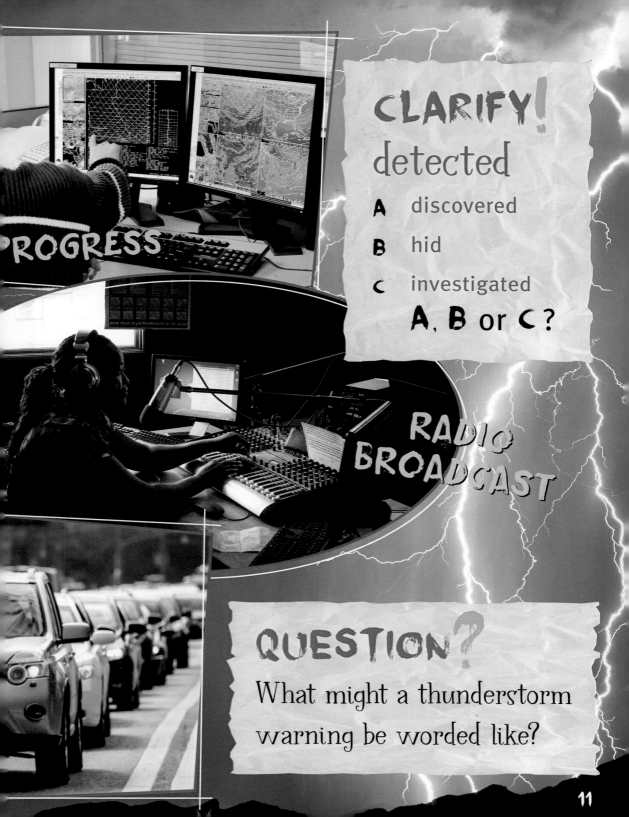

PROGRESS

CLARIFY!

detected

A discovered

B hid

C investigated

A, B or C?

RADIO BROADCAST

QUESTION?

What might a thunderstorm warning be worded like?

11

TORNADO!

Tornadoes are the most frightening of all weather alerts. Occasionally, a narrow, twisting column of air called a tornado may form from very severe thunderstorms (called 'supercells'). The column of air, or funnel, forms when a part of a thunderstorm starts to rotate. It twists at high speed, sucking things from the surface of the Earth into the air. The part of the tornado that touches the ground ranges in width from a few metres to a kilometre.

Measuring the speed of winds inside a tornado is very difficult, because the measuring instruments are often blown to pieces by the force of the wind! One of the highest wind speeds ever recorded in a tornado was 241 kilometres per hour in Michigan, United States of America, in 1965. It is thought that wind speeds in tornadoes may reach 500 kilometres per hour, and some meteorologists believe that speeds may even reach 800 kilometres per hour.

DEVASTATION

CLARIFY!

rotate

A twists

B moves in a circle

C moves up

A, **B** or **C**?

FIRE LINE DO NOT CROSS

FACT OR OPINION?

Tornadoes are the most frightening of all weather alerts.

Fact = A statement that can be proved to be true

Opinion = A view or belief that is not based on fact or knowledge

TORNADO CHASERS

Scientists do not fully understand why tornadoes form. Every tornado season, teams of scientists work in Tornado Alley, in the United States of America, studying tornadoes in the hope of finding out why they form. Once this is understood, scientists may be able to predict tornadoes earlier, so people have more warning.

When weather conditions are right for tornadoes to occur, meteorologists travel in large trucks that carry radar dishes. They follow severe thunderstorms, and if a tornado forms, they point their radar at it to study the speed and direction of the winds and to track the path of the tornado. Warnings are given so that people in the tornado's path can leave or find shelter.

EVACUATION ROUTE

STUDYING TORNADOES

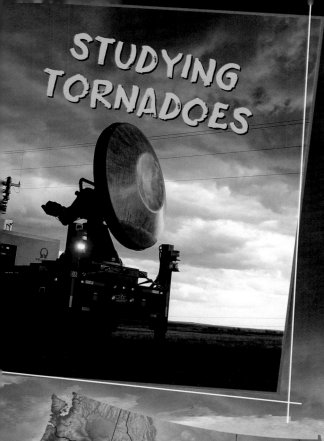

TORNADO ALLEY

Tornadoes occur in many parts of the world, but one part of the United States of America experiences more tornadoes than any other place. The low land stretching across the states of Texas, Oklahoma and Kansas is known as Tornado Alley. Cold, dry air flowing from the Rocky Mountains to the west often flows over moist, warm air flowing north from the Gulf of Mexico. This results in severe thunderstorms, some of which hatch tornadoes.

United States of America

MINNESOTA

SOUTH DAKOTA

WISCONSIN

WYOMING

NEBRASKA

IOWA

COLORADO

KANSAS

TORNADO ALLEY

NEW MEXICO

OKLAHOMA

TEXAS

CYCLONES, HURRICANES AND TYPHOONS

Cyclones are immense masses of swirling, moist air up to 600 kilometres across. They cause thunder, lightning, heavy rain and very high winds.

The air forms a huge spiral, which moves clockwise in the Southern Hemisphere and anticlockwise in the Northern Hemisphere. In the centre is a small, calm area of very low air pressure, called the 'eye'. The air moves faster as it approaches the eye, causing winds that may reach speeds of more than 250 kilometres an hour.

Anticlockwise

WHIRLPOOLS OF DESTRUCTION

whirlpools of destruction

What does this phrase mean?

NORTHERN HEMISPHERE

Equator

Clockwise

SOUTHERN HEMISPHERE

Meteorologists use satellite photographs and radar to watch for tropical cyclones forming far out to sea. Aircraft may also be sent to areas of low pressure to get an accurate air pressure measurement.

Once a tropical cyclone forms, its movement is tracked. Meteorologists try to predict when and where the tropical cyclone will cross the coast. If it appears that a large storm surge will cross the coast near a place where people live, the met service will issue a storm surge warning along with a cyclone warning. The very low air pressure in the centre of a cyclone causes the sea level to rise. During the most severe cyclones, the level of the sea may be up to 15 metres higher than normal. This is called a storm surge, a tidal surge or a tidal wave.

AND TYPHOONS

CYCLONE DESTRUCTION

STORM SURGE

TIDAL WAVE

INFORMATION

STORM SURGE

The height of a storm surge depends on many things:

- the strength of the cyclone (high winds will increase the height of the surge)
- the speed at which the cyclone is travelling (the faster the cyclone travels, the higher the surge)
- the shape of the land in the area (islands and headlands may funnel the surge, causing it to be higher)
- the height of the tide when the surge reaches the coast (the surge will be higher during high tide).

WEATHER DATA BANK

	SIZE (WIDTH)
TROPICAL CYCLONE	200 to 600 kilometres
NON-TROPICAL CYCLONE	500 to 1500 kilometres
THUNDERSTORM	500 to 2000 metres
TORNADO	100 to 1000 metres

EVENTS FACT FILE

USUAL WIND SPEED	LIFE SPAN	SEASON
100 to 200 kilometres per hour	5 to 10 days	Summer/autumn
50 to 100 kilometres per hour	5 to 10 days	Winter/spring
50 to 150 kilometres per hour	20 minutes to 2 hours	All seasons (more in spring and summer)
200 to 500 kilometres per hour	5 to 50 minutes	All seasons (more in spring and summer)

RANKING TORNADOES

RATING	WIND SPEED (KPH*)
F0	64 to 116 kph*
F1	117 to 180 kph*
F2	181 to 253 kph*
F3	254 to 332 kph*
F4	333 to 418 kph*
F5	over 418 kph*

* kph = kilometres per hour

INFORMATION

Tornadoes are ranked using the Fujita F-Scale. Meteorologists estimate the wind speed by looking at the amount of damage the tornado made.

WITH THE FUJITA F-SCALE

EXPECTED DAMAGE

Chimneys and windows damaged;
branches torn from trees

Roofs damaged; caravans tipped over;
cars pushed off roads

Roofs torn off houses; large trees snapped
or uprooted

Roofs and some walls torn from houses;
most trees uprooted

Most buildings destroyed; cars and other
heavy objects thrown through the air

Complete houses lifted into the air;
strong buildings destroyed

THE BEAUFORT WIND

NUMBER	DESCRIPTION	SPEED (KPH)
0	Calm	0–2
1	Light Air	3–6
2	Light Breeze	7–11
3	Gentle Breeze	12–19
4	Moderate Breeze	20–28
5	Fresh Breeze	29–38
6	Strong Breeze	39–49
7	Near Gale	50–61
8	Gale	62–74
9	Strong Gale	75–88
10	Storm	89–102
11	Violent Storm	103–117
12	Hurricane Force	118+

(adapted from NZ Met Service website)

SCALE (ON LAND)

COMMENTS

Smoke rises straight up

Smoke drifts

Wind felt on face; leaves rustle

Flags flap; twigs move all the time

Papers blow; small branches move

Small trees sway

Large branches move; wind whistles

Whole trees sway

Twigs break off; gale warning on radio

Large branches break; some damage occurs

Trees uprooted; major damage occurs

Danger – take shelter

Disastrous

GLOSSARY

electromagnetic   having the properties of electricity and magnetism

extreme   very great, intense

flash flooding   a sudden, violent flood

forecast   a prediction of future conditions

front   the line where two separate bodies of air meet

gust   a sudden, powerful burst of wind

meteorological   to do with weather and climate

meteorologist   a scientist who studies weather

microwave   a wave of electromagnetic energy, emitted by radar

precaution   something done to avoid a terrible or dangerous event

radar   a system that uses microwaves to detect the position and speed of storms

satellite   a device in space that collects and transmits information to Earth

severe   harsh, very bad, serious

storm surge   a dangerous rise in the level of the sea caused by a tropical cyclone

warning   information given about a dangerous event before it occurs

INDEX

Making connections – What connections
can you make with this text?

being perceptive to
changing conditions
weatherwise

conveying
serious
information
calmly

interpreting
information

Text to Self

able to
predict
events

being diligent
and alert

making
decisions

communicating
information to others

Text to Text

Talk about other informational texts you may have read that have similar features. Compare the texts.

Text to World

Talk about situations in the world that might connect to elements in the text.

PLANNING AN INFORMATIONAL REPORT

1 Organise the information

Select a topic

List the things you know and what things you will need to research

What I know:

Most communities have a met service.

Met services issue warnings about extreme weather events.

Extreme weather events tracked by met services include thunderstorms, tornadoes, cyclones, hurricanes and typhoons.

What I will research:

Who relies on the work of met services?

Why do met services issue warnings?

What part do radar play in tracking extreme weather events?

2 Locate the information you will need

Library

Internet

Experts

3 Process the information

Skim read.

Sort your ideas into groups.

Make some headings.

Plan the report

Write a general introduction.

5
Decide on a logical order for your information

What will come first, next ... last.

Write up your information

7
Design some visuals to include in your report

You can use: graphs, diagrams, labels, charts, tables, cross-sections ...

EVACUATION ROUTE

AN INFORMATIONAL REPORT

A Records information.

B Has no unnecessary descriptive details.

C Has no metaphors or similes.

D Uses scientific or technical terms.

E Uses the present tense.

F Is written in a formal style that is concise and accurate.

G Has a logical sequence of facts.

H Avoids author bias or opinion.